Table of Contents

Janelle R. Dawkins is The Resilient Mom Strategist, Coach, and Author who focuses on helping women develop strategies to bounce back after "Life Happens." She specializes in empowering women to dominate in her career field and at home. She has survived depression and low self-esteem, persevering through teenage parenthood and single motherhood. It is her mission to live out God's purpose for her life by helping women become more resilient and coach them to be bendable yet unbreakable under life's pressures.

Janelle is co-author of the book *Turbulence: A Practical Guide on How to Remain Resilient in The Midst of Life's Storms*, where she focuses on discussing her journey of overcoming turbulence: giving birth at fourteen, struggling academically at fifteen, and graduating from high school at sixteen with multiple college scholarships. Her assignment is to help inspire women and empower them to be strong like Titanium, letting go of the things that are keeping them from living their dreams and operating in God's purpose for their life.

Holding a Bachelor's degree in Biology from Salisbury University and a Master's degree in Management and Leadership from Liberty University, Janelle has over ten years of training and facilitating experience in several different industries. Janelle has been adding value to the industries she has worked in by training hundreds of people to follow their dreams, set goals, and be the best version of themselves. Her infectious personality has inspired others and has shifted the cultures of many workplace environments. Janelle has served as a role model to many working mothers around the country. She resides in Virginia with her husband and four children.

For more information please visit: www.theresilientmomstrategist.com
Email: janelle@theresilientmomstrategist.com
Address: P.O. Box 42, Onancock, VA 23417
Facebook: @Janelle Sampson Dawkins
Instagram: Janelle Dawkins
Periscope/Twitter: @JanelleDawkins

Relentless Hustle

Introduction

Jeremiah 29:11 states "For I know the plans I have for you," says the Lord. "They are plans for good and not for disaster, to give you a future and a hope."

Relentless hustle is the point at which you refuse to settle for less than what you want and what God has promised to you. It is when you have hit absolute rock bottom and you know there has to be more to life than what you are going through. I have had several relentless hustle moments in my life and they all usually were initiated by three simple words: I'll Show You. For years, it seemed like people were always doubting me, but now I know that I was being passive most of my life. I despised confrontation and simply rolled over for anything and anybody to avoid it. My relentless hustle felt like the fight of my life, especially if I felt as though my back was against the wall. Let me take you back to my first rock bottom moment where I had to hustle and pray to get out.

The year was 1992 and I was secretly a nerdy girl trying to fit in and be validated by the popular crowd. I grew up in a small town on the eastern shore of Maryland where our highlights were high school sports, lawn and house parties, and riding the bowl, which was nothing more than riding from the top of the "hill to the bottom and around by the shopping center" Oh the joys of county life. My town was an hour from DC and Baltimore, but I had heavy roots in both cities. It was never a problem to get a dose of the real city life when I wanted it. To this day, I credit my Baltimore family for my edginess. When I was fourteen, I became pregnant with my oldest son Jay. The crazy part about it was that I didn't know that I was pregnant or I tried really hard to believe I wasn't. I was a student athlete, so it was nothing for me to miss periods and this is what I thought had happened. I was very small for 5'10, so I didn't hardly gain any noticeable baby weight. I was in the 9th grade when I became pregnant with my son and I was about six months pregnant when I started to show. I didn't tell hardly anybody that I was pregnant because I didn't want to hear what they had to say.

This didn't resonate with me until recently when I connected with someone that I knew from high school. It was nice to hear that this individual had turned sour lemons into delicious lemonade and even built a few lemonade stands. What do I mean by that? Well, this person literally had nothing growing up and found a way to claw to the top to own and manage multiple seven-figure companies. Many things were going through my mind, but one question stood out the most: how did you get from point A to point B? It's different when you meet millionaires and you don't know their humble beginnings, but it's another thing when the last time you checked on a person, and all they were pulling out of their pockets was lint and living on student refunds, to now jet-setting across the world possessing hefty bank accounts; yes, you want to know the why and the how.

This book is designed to serve as a guide that will help you answer the tough "how to" questions, moving you from your current state to a more promising future state. This guide will take you on a journey to help you identify where you currently are in life and where you want to be. You will learn the strategies to press the reset button and detach from the people and things in your life that are keeping you stuck. Once you have completed this book, you will be able to recognize the indicators that tell you your environment is not conducive for growth. If you do the work, you will be able to face the issues in your life head-on and expose this world to your *Relentless Hustle*.

Day 1

Balance Is Not Harmony

People often strive to have work-life balance, but does that really exist? I learned some time ago that I wanted harmony because there are several moving parts in my life that all need to coexist in the same space. A different perspective on balance and harmony is listed below.

B- Be honest about what is really upsetting your life.

A- Allow yourself to let go of some things and people.

L- Learn a new way of thinking.

A- Allocate time for yourself.

N- Nothing is impossible.

C- Create a new routine.

E- Execute the plan you have set for yourself.

H- Hammer out your most dreaded task first.

A- Agree to disagree.

R- Refuse to give up when things get rough.

M- Mimic and multiply the things that are working in your life.

O- Observe your surroundings for inspiration.

N- Nurture the process.

Y- Yearn for consistency.

<u>Self-Evaluation Questions</u>

1. What aspects of my life require balance and harmony?

_____

_____

_____

2. Who is involved in helping me achieve balance and harmony?

_____

_____

_____

3. What are some of the challenges to obtaining balance and harmony?

_____

_____

_____

4. What are some wins in my quest for balance and harmony?

_____

_____

_____

Day 2

Know Where Your Time Is Going

Identify what it is that has you feeling overwhelmed.

If you are on the move running around like a "chicken with its head cut off," then this is the perfect place for you to start. Have you ever just had more chores/tasks/errands than you had time to do them in? Yeah me too, and I had to stop and identify what it was I was doing that seemed to make everyone else happy, but had me feeling like I was the craziest person ever.

Fill out the table below with what a typical seven-day week may look like for you. Add the total number of hours per day you devote to each item. Please be honest with yourself; this will identify the areas that are demanding your time and causing the imbalance in your life.

Total Number Of Hours You Spend On Activities							
	Sun	Mon	Tue	Wed	Thu	Fri	Sat
Working							
Cleaning							
Children							
Organizations							
Church							
Spouse							
You							
Household							

Self-Evaluation Questions

1. Did you discover the areas that are demanding the bulk of your time?

_____

_____

_____

2. Have you evaluated the areas where you can eliminate wasted time?

_____

_____

_____

3. Are there areas that you feel you spend the correct amount of time in?

_____

_____

_____

Day 3

Overwhelmed No More, Take Command of Your Life

Find the opportunity to dedicate time just for you! It's ok to start off small; for instance, focus on one hour a week and work your way up to one hour a day. I use the following strategy to organize my weekly routine to take back command over my life:

Motivational Monday: Use this day to listen and read all things motivational. The reality is that   often times, we have to motivate our own selves.

Transformational Tuesday: Use this day to transform your mind, body, soul, and home. Go to the gym or redecorate. Did you know most retail stores do markdowns on this day? Try a new recipe or a new hairdo. Make today totally about doing something different that will create a physical, spiritual or emotional transformation in your life.

Wellness Wednesday: Use this day to make all doctor appointments and meal prep. If you are still in the working world, then leaving early on "Hump Day" makes the weekend just that much closer. Meal prep helps you to foster better eating habits, especially if you are a mom that is constantly on the go.

Thankful Thursday: Reflect on the things that you are thankful for. Find a quiet area to pray and meditate.

Fun Friday: Have fun with your family. Have an in-house game night or head out to your favorite restaurant for dinner.

Self-Care Saturday: This is the day you do something special for you! Just remember: you do not always have to spend money to do something special for you. If you are a mom that is always on the go, welcome the idea of just having a quiet movie night at home alone.

Sanctified Sports Sunday: This day is for the Lord and sports (LOL). Can you tell I am a sports junkie who loves the Lord? If I am away from my home church, I am determined to get the message someway, somehow.

Plan your weekly schedule to take back command over your life.

Day	Primary Activity	Secondary Activity	Self-Care Activity
_____ Monday			
_____ Tuesday			
_____ Wednesday			
_____ Thursday			
_____ Friday			
_____ Saturday			
_____ Sunday			

Day 4

Triggers

We all have things that will send us over the mental edge if we are not careful. You know how you give your children that final warning, like "Look, if I have to tell you one more time you are going to know it," and then magically, it gets quiet and you now have peace because they know you are serious? Or, if your husband or significant other does that thing you hate *one more time* you're going to snap? How about after you clean the house only to return home to the same cluttered mess you had before you cleaned it? These, my friend, are triggers.

Trigger, in this sense, can be defined as "something that acts like a mechanical trigger in initiating a process or reaction" (Merriam Webster dictionary).

Today, I want you to create a list of the top ten triggers that drastically alter your mood or create a shift in your spirit.

Top 10 Triggers

1. _____
2. _____
3. _____
4. _____
5. _____
6. _____
7. _____
8. _____
9. _____
10. _____

Day 5

Deactivating the Triggers

Yesterday, you identified the top ten things that can make you turn into the Nutty Professor and today, you will take the necessary steps to deactivate them by applying your ABC's.

A- Alert the individual that their behavior/action (trigger) is bothering you.

Most of the time, people don't know they are triggering a negative emotion in you because they are not you, even if they perform the action repeatedly.

B- Be kind and considerate in your delivery. You know the saying: "It's not what you say—it's how you say it."

Even if you have reached your limit, there is no need to be rude or take your frustration out on another individual.

C- Calculate your steps. Have a plan in place to maneuver around the triggers and destress before you try to handle them head-on.

If you know your child has to practice their instrument and it completely gets on your nerves, then choose another activity to do that will get you away while your child is practicing.

Here is a sample script you can use when trying to deactivate triggers:

"I have noticed that you have been (fill in the action/behavior), and it has caused some uneasiness with me. Can we please find a way to resolve this matter that causes us both the least amount of discomfort?"

Day 6

Consistency

Congratulations! You have made it to day 6! To achieve your goals, you have to consistently follow-through with your actions.

Set one goal for the next twenty-four hours and make a list of five steps that you can do throughout the day to help you accomplish this goal. Be sure to schedule each of the steps at different times of the day, and keep notes on what works and what didn't work.

Step 1:
_____
_____

Step 2:
_____
_____

Step 3:
_____
_____

Step 4:
_____
_____

Step 5:

_____

_____

Takeaways: List what worked and what didn't work.

Day 7

Distractions

A distraction is something that prevents someone from dedicating their undivided attention to something else, and this world is full of them. People are often distracted by social media, television, smartphones, and let's not forget humans and pets. This will be a two-part challenge for you to first identify what you spend your time on, then to uncover the meaningless task(s) that are distracting you.

Track your day: <u>using the next 24 hours, try your absolute best to record every minute of your day.</u> If you are going to the bathroom, log it. If you take a social media break, log this as well. Do not try to round up time or combine tasks. Believe me: this is very important in helping you identify what the major distractions are in your life.

Part I: During the first hour of this exercise, on a separate sheet of paper, write down as many examples of distractions you can think of. Save this list for later because we will come back to it.

Part II:

ACTIVITY	TIME START	TIME END

Self-Evaluation Questions

1. What is your number one distraction?

   _____

   _____

   _____

   _____

2. How will you remove this distraction?

   _____

   _____

   _____

   _____

3. What surprised you about the results of this activity?

   _____

   _____

   _____

   _____

Day 8

Write A Letter To Your Younger Self

My journey to resilience began when I was a scared, naïve young girl out in the streets doing grown-up things that I was not ready for. I had no idea what my actions would cause me to have to deal with head-on later in life. If you would have asked me back then, I would have proclaimed to be the "Give-up" strategist—not the Resilient Mom strategist. Write a letter to your younger self, giving her some of the advice you wished someone would have told you. This activity will shed some insight on the things that you may be having difficulty with, keeping you from dominating at work and home.

_____

_____

_____

_____

_____

_____

_____

_____

_____

_____

_____

_____

_____

_____

_____

_____

_____

Day 9

This Is Just A Test

I find it amazing the things that women actually go through in life. I heard a teaching on the Proverbs 31 man and the Proverbs 31 woman where the roles in the relationship were clearly defined. This teaching spelled out what a Kingdom Man and Kingdom Woman should look like. This message really resonated with me because before then, I really didn't know what these roles were supposed to look like. I learned that it is not my role to reaffirm a man's confidence. I learned that if I'm going to be a Proverbs 31 woman *about my business*, then I need a Proverbs 31 man that is *about his business*. Nowhere in this passage is there an insecure woman or an insecure man. When you have either of the two, your relationship is simply out of order.

How can you have a solid relationship when there is no trust and it's filled with insecurity? I talk about the issue of people-pleasing, and how for years, I was an avid people-pleaser. I wanted to make sure everybody was happy all the time, and many people used whatever manipulative tricks and tools to get me to do what they wanted me to do. It didn't happen overnight, but I finally woke up and stopped letting people manipulate me. Now, I can't stand for that! My current expectations shifted: in order for you to deal with me, you have to be a secure person. I refuse to shrink back to that insecure little girl that I once was, because you're playing small does not serve the world.

Now where is the test? The test comes in just when you think you have mastered your issues. The test is when you have successfully passed all the quizzes, such as paying all your bills on time, conquering lust, and managing your emotions. Just when you think you have healed from all the hurt and bitterness you have been harboring, here comes the test. What are some things that you have been tested with?

Self-Evaluation Question

1. Have you been truthful with yourself?

   _____

   _____

   _____

   _____

2. Was there anything that surprised you?

   _____

   _____

   _____

   _____

3. What is the one thing that keeps reoccurring?

   _____

   _____

   _____

   _____

What are the opportunities testing you?	What triggers this test?	Why do you keep letting it effect you?	What can you do differently to overcome this test for good?
1. Bitterness	When people don't do what they say they are going to do.	Because it creates more work for me.	Learn to be more self-sufficient.
2.			
3.			
4.			
5.			
6.			

Day 10

Check Your Environment

Your surroundings or environment is very impactful to your life. Take for instance, a houseplant that is all of a sudden beginning to turn yellow. This plant started as a simple leaf in a glass of water. For months, the plant was thriving in the water, but began to indicate there was a problem with its' yellow tint. Why do you think this is? Well, you guessed right: the plant was no longer thriving in its environment.

Plants are not the only ones that produce indicators as a response to triggers within their environment. When something is going on in your environment such as stress, your body may give the indication that a change is needed by giving you a headache. In the case of the plant, it's giving me an indicator letting me know it is time for a change by turning yellow and losing its beautiful green color. This is the plant screaming at me, "Hey! Something is wrong; I don't like my environment, and it is time for me to go into the dirt." So, what's the message here? Take a look at yourself and evaluate whether or not you are thriving and growing in your current environment.

Self- Evaluation Questions:

1. Describe your current work environment. Are there any indicators in your current work environment that may suggest you need a change?

   _____
   _____
   _____
   _____
   _____
   _____

2. If there were no restrictions, what sort of environment would you like to work in? Describe your dream job (company name, location, and other details).

_____
_____
_____
_____
_____
_____

3. Describe your current home environment. Are there any indicators in your current home environment that may suggest you need a change?

_____
_____
_____
_____
_____
_____

4.   If there were no restrictions, what sort of environment would you like to live in? Describe your dream house, and where it is located.

_____
_____
_____
_____
_____
_____

Day 11

It's Time to Become Fearless

Fear stands for **Facing Everything Abducting Rewards**, and that is just what you have to do with the things that are stopping you from getting to your next level. Fear can literally stop you in your tracks and stop you from doing the things that God has destined you to do. Fear will keep you stuck in the box that is disguised as your dead-end job, toxic relationship, or situation you know you shouldn't be in. There are usually red flags when fear is lurking around you, and it's up to you to pay attention.

My brush with fear began as a young girl. I was fearful that I wasn't pretty enough, smart enough, athletic enough, or popular enough. This fear of not being "enough" became the continuous IV to the habit of people-pleasing I developed, but we will talk about that a little later.

In column one, write down every fear you have ever had. In column two, write down the corresponding reason why you had this fear or where it originated from (i.e. fear of cats because of a painful scratch). Use an additional piece of paper if needed.

Fear	Reason Why

Day 12

Breaking The Curse Of Codependency

In my lifetime, I have stayed in situations way longer than I should have because I thought I needed that man, financial source, or job to survive. I am so glad I can say that when you know better, you do better! I know now that all I needed was God on my side in order to achieve the impossible. I remember taking my first leap of faith to breaking codependency. I was a single mother of my three oldest children at the time, fighting what I thought was the battle of my life. I found myself in the middle of a bitter custody battle with my youngest children's father. For years, we fought over everything, especially money. We fought for so long that I ended up with forty thousand dollars' worth of legal bills, family turmoil, embarrassment, and enough stress to make a person have a stroke and heart attack.

Why does someone deal with that type of stress and strain? Because they feel they have to. When you are dealing with codependency, you develop a pattern of messing up, getting into jams, then "Captain Save'em" sweeps in and saves the day. "Captain Save'em" is equal to your inhibitor. You think they are helping you by coming to your rescue, but what they are really causing you to do is to depend on them more for the solutions to your problems.

Today is going to take some real courage and honesty on your part! This is the only way you will be able to truly break the cycle of codependency.

Self-Evaluation Questions

1. Write down all the areas in your life that you ask people to come to your rescue.

    _____
    _____
    _____
    _____

2. Write down the specific instances that someone came to your rescue.

_____

_____

_____

_____

3. How did they specifically help you in the instances listed in question number 2?

_____

_____

_____

_____

4. How did you get in these predicaments? What were your next steps after they saved you?

_____

_____

_____

_____

5. What have you done in the last 30 days to not depend on someone else for a need that you had?

_____

_____

_____

_____

6. What will you do in the next 30 days to break the cycle of codependency? How will you change your mindset to be more self-sufficient in the next 30 days? (HINT: Formulate your strategy!)

_____

_____

_____

_____

I know that the future seems bleak when you don't know where your solution is going to come from. This will help you untie the apron strings that are keeping you tied and feeling stuck to the dependent source.

Day 13

Believe You Can Do It

"You will never be able to help anyone else until you help yourself," was the statement that echoed in my head over and over during the fall of 2015. My therapist told me this as I sat on her couch telling her what I really wanted to do with my life. I kept asking myself, *"What did she means by this?"* In my head, I had it all together. I knew that I wanted to help women in my same situation gain confidence and courage to break free from toxic situations. As usual, my response was *I'll show you*, but this time, my attempts at showing my therapist didn't come to fruition until much later. I continued on my quest to help others as my world was crumbling down around me. I had enrolled in a second Master's program to be a licensed marriage and family counselor, but my marriage was a mess. I psyched myself out because I didn't believe I could be a marriage counselor or fix my marriage. All it takes is one seed of negativity to be planted to overtake your life. But it also takes one seed of positivity to get you on the right track.

Today, you are going to shift your mindset! List the top five things you want to accomplish and below them write an "I believe I can statement." My life did not turn around until I believed that it could. You can do it!

I want to accomplish:

1. _____

    I believe I can

    _____

    _____

2. _____

    I believe I can

    _____

    _____

3. _____

   I believe I can

   _____

   _____

4. _____

   I believe I can

   _____

   _____

5. _____

   I believe I can

   _____

   _____

Day 14

Write A Letter Of Encouragement To Your Current Self

Let's face it: sometimes you have to encourage YOURSELF! On days when I have been in a funk (yes that does happen to me LOL), I pull out my old journals and read where I used to be and the encouragement and hope that I gave to myself to know that things would soon be different. Write a letter to yourself praising the progress you have made and giving hope for the future. Claim your victory; if you do the work, it will happen!

You are making great strides to dominate in your home and work life! Keep going and remember that RESILIENT WOMEN KEEP GETTING UP!

_____
_____
_____
_____
_____
_____
_____
_____
_____
_____
_____
_____
_____
_____
_____
_____
_____
_____
_____
_____
_____

Day 15

Getting Out Of Neutral

Have you ever been trying to move your car forward by pressing on the gas, but your car simply will not move and you look down at the gear shaft and realize you put it in neutral instead of drive? This happens in life sometimes where you feel like you are just simply stuck and you desire to move forward, but you don't know how.

Reveal

Revealing the things that are keeping you stuck in neutral is the first step to moving forward.

Take a minute to ask yourself what are the top 3 things that keep you from taking steps in the direction you want to go? Is it lack of time or money? Are you short on motivation? Is your life cluttered and complicated? Or do you give everything you have to everyone but yourself? Write them below.

1. _____
   _____
2. _____
   _____
3. _____
   _____

Identifying what is holding you back is key to your forward momentum....

Target

Now that you have identified the top 3 things that are keeping you stuck, now it is time to narrow your focus in on these items and turn them from challenges to motivation for change.

How will I do things differently?

_____

_____

_____

_____

Action

When you hear the words *"Lights, camera, action!"* you know something is about to take place. Webster's dictionary defines action as "a thing done." When you say you are going to take action, do just that and follow-through. Taking action leads to results and results allow you to measure change and growth. People often say "I'm going to pray about it," but God requires much more than that. God can only take you but so far! James 2:17 says "In the same way, faith by itself, if it is not accompanied by action, is dead" (NIV).

Getting out of neutral will require you to identify the top things that are keeping you stuck in your current state. Once you know what these things are, then develop a plan to change them from challenges to motivators. Lastly, it is time to put your plan in motion and take action to obtaining the positive results to move you forward to your goals.

What results do I want to achieve?

_____

_____

_____

_____

_____

_____

_____

Day 16

Diary of A Control Freak

I'm sure we all know someone who has to be in control of every single aspect except their own life. If using fictional characters as an example, this person would share characteristics with Mary Jane Paul from The BET series *"Being Mary Jane"* or Veronica Harrington from Tyler Perry's *"The Have and The Have Nots."* These two women appear to have it all together on the outside, but are silently suffering on the inside, hence the need to control.

Here are 5 tips to identify if you are a control freak:

1. You have all the answers. Control freaks feel they are among the smartest people in the room, if not the smartest. Now I'm not saying all people that think this way are control freaks; this is just one of the characteristics.

2. Their way is the best way or the only way. There are several different ways to get to the beach just because you ride a bike every time does not discard the method of walking. Each route has their positives and negatives but you will always end up in the same place.

3. They do not like to hear the word NO. Control freaks have a problem with this word and anyone that says this word to them. They usually try and avoid the word NO at all costs. Surrounding themselves with people-pleasers, control freaks are less likely to hear the word NO, and are able to operate in an environment where they are most comfortable.

4. They lack transparency. Control freaks always want to know what you are doing, but hardly ever share anything about themselves. Their need to be in the know is so that they can ensure they are still the smartest person in the room. If they feel like you have a slight edge on them, knowing your moves will allow them to study the area they are lacking.

5. Their tone is condescending. Control freaks oftentimes talk to you like you're stupid. Even when they try to be polite, they lack that sense of authenticity.

I know I covered a lot, but if you have any of these characteristics, this could be why you are not dominating in the areas you desire to operate in. Today, reflect on a time when you worked with someone from your home or work life to complete a task. Evaluate your performance during this process, and note if you displayed any characteristics of control. Write them below.

_____

_____

_____

_____

_____

Day 17

The Soundtrack Of Your Life—What Emotions Inspire You

This exercise will help you think about the songs that inspire you to take action in your life. Have you ever heard a song and it took you back to the exact place and time that you first heard it or it brought back a fond memory? Well, I have songs that motivate and inspire me to make it happen. This is something that you may have never thought of before. Please look at the example provided and then complete the chart by adding songs that affect your emotions.

Title/ Artist	Your Feeling/Mood	What Is The Memory?	Why Did You Choose This Song?
Jazmine Sullivan-Bust The Windows Out Your Car	Fed up and not taking it anymore	Cheating boyfriends	It inspired me to send a powerful message
Ledisi & Kirk Franklin – If You Don't Mind	Happy, Free & at Peace	Letting God lead my life.	It's okay to try it God's way.

Day 18

Sometimes You Have To Press the Reset Button

It's never too late to start over or get a fresh start. Today, you are going to press the reset button in your relationships, your goals, and your faith. Even if you fail, fail forward on that reset button: get up and start again. I failed this week at my exercise goals; I had my systems in place to meet it, but I didn't. Of course, I wanted to give up, but I pressed that reset button and started charging forward to the goal at hand. You never know what you're really made of until you push yourself. I have been spending time at my daughter-in-law's school, and it reminded me of my college years, and the fight that it took for me to overcome some obstacles to obtain my degree. I had to start over many times and push myself to make it to school because I wanted better for my children. I was a single mother trying to make it and that required me to start over many times. I was thankful for every clean slate (opportunity) I was given. I want you all to understand that anything is possible. Sometimes, you just need to press the reset button and give yourself a little push. What are the top five things that motivate you to press the reset button, helping you to focus on your goals?

1. _____
2. _____
3. _____
4. _____
5. _____

<u>Self- Evaluation Questions</u>

1. How do I press reset and jump-start the goals I have for my life?

_____

_____

_____

_____

_____

2. Write down a plan that will help you stay committed to what you have written down.

_____

_____

_____

_____

_____

Day 19

Embrace It

One of the biggest struggles I had throughout my life, was embracing qualities and characteristics that I possess. For three years in a row, I was required to take a personality assessment at a conference for work. Over time, my scores showed improvement because I was actually participating in my own personal development journey, but in one area, I got the same results year in and year out. I scored high in the area of persuasion and sales. I immediately thought this wasn't right because I was one of the nicest, most passive people you could meet. In my mind, people that scored high in these areas were sharks. The last year that I took the assessment, the instructor pulled me aside and said "Hey Janelle, this doesn't have to be a bad thing; you simply have to embrace it." It wasn't until then that I decided to turn what I thought was negative into a positive and began to use it for my good.

During my time in network marketing, I could easily meet and exceed sales goals due to my gift of sales, but I was in denial. Embracing the quality of salesmanship has actually helped me as an entrepreneur. It was one of the skills that kicked into high gear when *Relentless Hustle* was required for me to provide for my children as a single mother. As time went on, I discovered other qualities within me that I needed to embrace, and you will too!

Self-Evaluation Questions

1. Name three things that you are in denial of embracing.

    1. _____

    2. _____

    3. _____

2. Are you ashamed of these things? Explain.

_____

_____

_____

_____

_____

3. What are you going to do differently to embrace and develop these qualities?

_____

_____

_____

_____

_____

Day 20

Your Life's Strategic Plan

People have good ideas all day every day, but in order for those ideas to work, there is one key component needed: strategy. I consider myself a smart person, but I learned a lot of hard lessons because I lacked strategy. I tried to do things my way and not God's way. Before you start to think about a strategic plan for your life, pray this simple prayer with me:

"Lord help me to see me the way You see me." Now you're ready to set a strategy for your life.

S- Surrender to God's dream for yourself

T- Take time for yourself

R-Reality check (evaluate what's limiting you)

A- Accountability for your actions, progress, and results

T- Tap into what you are good at

E- Embrace it (your qualities)

G-Give it to God and let Him lead the way

Y-Your "YES" is required to activate the plan

Use the space below to create a strategic plan for your life. Include your mission, vision, and goals. Also include where you see yourself in the next year, five years, and ten years.

_____
_____
_____
_____
_____
_____
_____
_____
_____
_____

Day 21

SWOT Your Life

A SWOT analysis is a tool used in business that primarily acts as a planning method that evaluates the Strengths, Weaknesses, Opportunities, and Threats within an organization. You are going to apply this tool to your life to help you identify the areas that need attention.

Strengths- What am I good at?	**Weaknesses**- What are the weaknesses in my life?
Opportunities- What can I work on?	**Threats**- What is in the way?

Day 22

Focus

Relentless Hustle takes FOCUS! If you ask anybody that has had any sort of success, they will tell you that you have to place your eyes on the prize and go get it! If you take your eyes off of the target for just one second, it can be gone—just like that. I asked one of my childhood friends how he went from living in a foster home to being a wealthy business man with a whole lot of failures and disappointments along the way. His response: "I focused on what I wanted and didn't let any obstacles get in the way." I was thinking, *That's it?* This was a moment of inspiration for me because I watched this same person earn a full college scholarship in a sport he had only been playing for three years.

Philippians 3:15 MSG says "So let's keep focused on that goal, those of us who want everything God has for us. If any of you have something else in mind, something less than total commitment, God will clear your blurred vision - you'll see it yet!"

F-Find out what you want
O- Overcome the obstacles that stand in your way
C-Center in on your goal and chase it
U-Use the skills and resources you already have
S-Stay the course and don't get distracted. Start small; even if you move an inch, you are still moving.

Self- Evaluation Questions

1. What are some things you can do to refocus on your goal when you lose focus?

_____

_____

_____

_____

2. Pick three different times today that you will think about your goal and nothing else. Write the time in the first column and mark the completed column when it's done.

Time	Completed

Day 23

Bypassing Bitterness

Are you a "Bitter Betty," or do you know a "Bitter Betty?" I described in earlier parts of the book about my long, drawn out custody battle with my children's father. This situation made me very bitter. I had a victim's mentality and no accountability for the part I played in the matter. Bitterness can actually suck the life out of you, stunt your growth, and steal your focus right from underneath you. When you're bitter, you are the only one right, and you want to win at all costs. Bitterness is that feeling in the pit of your stomach when you see someone and you are still mad and you don't know why. In order to bypass your bitterness, you need to let it go. I know it's easier said than done, but I'm here to tell you that once you release bitterness, so many other doors will open up. Referring back to the child custody issue I had, I actually lost $40,000 over being bitter. I could've done so much more with that money if I had been happy. But I was on a quest to be right with my bitter self.

Bypassing bitterness is going to allow you to do a couple of things:

1. Bring maturity to your life.
2. Allow you to focus on your goals and create strategies for you to accomplish your goals.
3. Reduce distractions.

Bitterness is a major distraction. Letting it go allows you to make better decisions at work and for your family. Let's talk about bitterness in your career. I know I talk a lot about home life, but bitterness is alive and well in the workplace too. Every office has that one employee that keeps all the mess going on in the office. This person has usually been there for some time and has been passed over for promotions in the past. If you have experienced this person, you already know that you cannot and will not change them. But if you hang around them long enough, they will infect you with their bitterness.

There is no self-evaluation today; I just want you to write a pledge to yourself in your own words about how you will be bypassing bitterness from here on out.

_____
_____
_____
_____
_____
_____
_____
_____
_____
_____
_____
_____
_____
_____
_____
_____
_____
_____

Day 24

Mastering Your Self-Esteem

How we feel about ourselves is definitely a learned behavior. Depending on what you've been exposed to determines ultimately how you feel about yourself. When I was younger, I was categorized as selfish and instead of embracing it, I tried hard to prove to people that I was not selfish. I talked in some detail about my past self-esteem issues in the book *Turbulence*. Being a teenage parent constantly made me feel as though I was not good enough. Teenage parenthood was something that wasn't promoted in any culture, and people didn't hesitate to let me know their disapproval. Although I took care of my outer appearance, I definitely hid behind the mask of poor self-esteem.

Today, we're going to make two columns. In column one, write all of your traits that make you feel good about yourself. In column two, write all of the negative things you feel about yourself. Which column has more items?

Self-Examination Questions

1. In two sentences, describe yourself in a positive way.

_____
_____
_____
_____

2. In two sentences, describe how you think others view you.

_____
_____
_____
_____

3. If you could change one thing about yourself, what would it be and why?

_____
_____
_____
_____

Day 25

Affirmations That Win

Affirmations are statements that you declare to be true. Affirmations helped me get through one of the lowest points in my life. I literally had to speak life into myself because I was surrounded by people that were trying to kill my dreams and spirit with the words they were saying to me. Below are a few of the affirmations that I used to speak life into myself to overcome one of my darkest hours. I encourage you to develop your own affirmation based on your life.

1. I am an overcomer.
2. I deserve God's best for my life.
3. I am an awesome mother, and my children love and appreciate me.
4. I am a money magnet, wealth is in my present and my future.
5. I am in control of my actions, emotions, and my time.
6. I am a go-getter and my success is equal to my results.
7. I am who God says I am, public opinion does not make me.

Write your affirmations below, and feel free to add to the list as you think of them.

_____
_____
_____
_____
_____
_____
_____
_____
_____
_____
_____
_____
_____
_____
_____
_____

Day 26

Settling Spirits

I often get asked why do I live where I live, work where I work and have relationships with people that just don't seem like a good fit. I have been known to "play it safe" in many occasions and that is nothing but a limiting behavior. You have to be careful not to limit yourself in order to please others. Live out loud every opportunity you get. There are people that I have been associated with that have tried to belittle me just to make themselves look good. If someone has to do this to another person, then that means you intimidate and threaten them by your very existence. I settled for this type of behavior for fear of being alone and wanting to fit into a group. I was on a quest to find a companion that enjoyed my time, enjoyed church, and had a good heart, but I would soon learn that the nice "corny" guys couldn't believe that I was even talking to them. They wanted to parade me around like those NFL players who just won the Super Bowl trophy. A tip to keep in mind is that you make the clothes, they don't make you, and that goes for relationships also.

How do you know if you have a settling spirit? You know you have a settling spirit if you just do things to keep the peace in your home. If you are typically passive on issues and do not like confrontation, then you have a settling spirit. If you put up with poor treatment and deal with people and things that do not honor you as a person, then you have a settling spirit.

People settle when they are trying to avoid the very things they think they cannot have. People also settle when they are not patient; they say yes to the first train coming. People settle just to keep up with appearances. No more settling; it's time to be honest.

Have you ever settled for anything in your life? Warning: the answer may be something you did not want to admit, but as the saying goes, tell the truth and shame the devil.

_____

_____

_____

_____

_____

_____

_____

_____

_____

_____

_____

_____

_____

_____

_____

_____

_____

_____

_____

_____

_____

_____

Day 27

Financial Check

There is a millionaire calling on my life, but I can't claim it by being wasteful, spending money like crazy. We all have some sort of financial habit that is stopping us from getting to our next millionaire opportunity. I am bold enough to be transparent and tell you mine is spending.

When your "money is funny and your change is strange," there are only two things you can do: fight to fix it; or tuck, run, and hide. Let's be honest: when our finances are out of order, most times we are too. You don't just wake up one morning and say, "Hey, I'm going to be broke today, and as a matter of fact, I'm going to be broke forever." That simply does not happen. The behaviors, habits, and bad choices that we make continue to keep our finances in a fragile state. If I can have a moment of transparency, I knew the exact point when my finances went from broke to broken. I actually accumulated debt at the age of 16. I was a college freshman and in the early nineties, the credit card companies were allowed to camp out in student centers soliciting victims with the things broke, hungry, college freshmen wanted. Let me further set the stage for you. I was two states from home, on a super-fixed zero-budget with *absolutely* no money for candy and snacks that I so desired to have. So of course, if you dangle what an immature sixteen-year-old wanted in her face, she is most certainly going to take the bait. I took the bait from many companies during my freshman year—all before my 18th birthday.

I hear so many women complain about two things: time and MONEY. Today, we are going to create a basic budget to help you check your finances. The key here is discipline!

One of the greatest lessons I have ever learned about money is that of compound interest. "A dollar saved today is worth more than a dollar saved tomorrow." In my early twenties, when I would leave a job, I thought my 401K payout was a bonus check... I know... funny right?

Make a list of your expenses and subtract this amount from your total income. If this number is positive, ask yourself if you are happy with this number. Is it enough to live the life you want? If the answer is no, then you need to do something different to get a different result. If this number is negative, then you got to do something different for another reason. It is time for you to pray then hustle relentlessly to change that negative into a positive. Keep working at it!

Day 28

Relationship Goals

A man will notice your beauty long before he says anything to you. Just know that you are being watched at all times, and when a man truly wants to be with you, he will take the necessary steps to keep you in his life. Men can recognize a quality woman and a scandalous woman at any time. Men know what they want; they just may have trouble expressing it at times. Women, on the other hand, can easily communicate what they don't want, but hardly ever communicate what it is they do want. Throughout this book, the consistent theme is strategy. This also applies to your relationships.

In this exercise, you will identify what qualities you want in a man and what you want your relationship to look like.

MY IDEAL MAN

- SPIRITUAL ATTRIBUTES
- PHYSICAL ATTRIBUTES
- FINANCIAL ATTRIBUTES
- FAMILY VALUES
- RELATIONSHIP GOALS
- DEAL BREAKERS

_____
_____
_____
_____
_____
_____
_____
_____
_____

Day 29

Have Some "Atta Girl" Moments

I know like most women and mothers, we are great at celebrating everyone else, but have a difficult time celebrating ourselves. We minimize our accomplishment and provide several excuses as to why we cannot take the time to pat our own selves on the back. In the American culture, we celebrate the milestones of our children—sometimes with over-the-top celebrations with ease. We encourage them and give them an "Atta girl," keep up the good work (at least in the country LOL) as they learn to crawl, walk, and even ride a bike. In the teenage years, things start to change and young ladies hear more critiques than "Atta girls." In adulthood, people will celebrate milestones, but their celebrations are often followed with negativity and discouragement.

A shift needs to occur! Celebrating yourself and others builds confidence, creates momentum, and acknowledges results. Say this poem out loud on a daily until it sticks.

I Am My Biggest Competition

She is not in charge of my destiny,

It is me who determines all that I can be.

Milestones are to be celebrated at best,

Whether I know her, or like her she deserves an "Atta Girl" when she passes that test.

There is enough hate all around the world then to continue to spread any negativity, know and understand that your sister is not the enemy.

My only competition in this world is ME!

Celebrate your wins so the world can see, Confidence, Momentum, and Results are your God given destiny.

My wins for today are:

_____

_____

_____

_____

_____

_____

_____

_____

_____

_____

_____

_____

Day 30

Write A Letter Of Encouragement To Your Future Self

You have made it! I hope that you have found this book helpful in your quest to dominate your home and work life. Just because you have reached the end of the book doesn't mean the work is finished. You have to keep setting goals and keep making progress to achieving the results you want. On this last day, you will write a letter to your future self, encouraging her to keep praying and keep going. DREAM BIG and then let God show you the plan to get there. You will have this letter to refer back to in the future in order to have a tangible measurement of how much you have grown.

You will dominate in your home and work-life from this day forward! I believe in you, and remember that RESILIENT WOMEN keep getting up!

_____

_____

_____

_____

_____

_____

_____

_____

_____

_____

_____

_____

_____

_____

_____

_____

_____

_____

_____

Acknowledgement

I first want to thank my Heavenly Father for giving me the courage, wisdom, knowledge, and passion to help the people that will be impacted by this book. My life has not been the same since I have said yes to Him and committed to doing the necessary work on me! This holds true for you as well.

As the saying goes it takes a village, well that has been the case with this project! My village has been in the trenches with me during this project from helping with the children to covering my family in prayer. I want to thank my husband Jibreel for picking up the slack when I was in full writing mode. I want to thank my children Brynden, Lyric, Akilah, and Jennah for respecting mommy's work time and eating more takeout than usual during the creation of this book. Special thanks goes to Carla Cannon for pushing me when I didn't want to be pushed and activating what God had placed on inside of me. My Publishing, editing and creative team has made this process exceptionally smooth! Thank you to Kiyanni Bryan with Write It Out Publishing, Katherine A. Young Editorial Services, Jason Josiah with Living Word Illustration, and Kirk Hynson of Hyson's Photo Services, I can't wait to work with you all again.

A special thank you goes to the numerous family members, church members, and friends that have supported me along the way, I am forever grateful.

Be blessed and *Hustle Relentlessly* to the greatness God has for you!

Janelle

www.ingramcontent.com/pod-product-compliance
Lightning Source LLC
LaVergne TN
LVHW061229060426
835509LV00012B/1478